Piecing Life Together
Creatively through Quilting

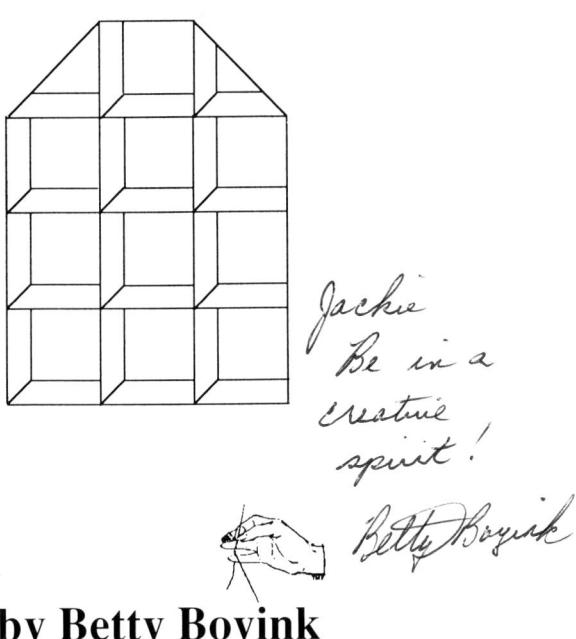

Jackie
Be in a
creative
spirit!

Betty Boyink

by Betty Boyink

All rights reserved. No part of this book may be reproduced in any form without written permission from Betty Boyink Publishing.

ISBN 0-926523-06-07

Please try to purchase at book store or quilt shop. Book may be ordered by mail from publisher. Please add $3.50 shipping and handling. Wholesale inquiries welcome.

Copyright 1996
Betty Boyink Publishing
818 Sheldon Road
Grand Haven, MI 49417
FAX 616-842-3327

Printed in Hong Kong

Dedicated to the Memory

of my parents,
Ethel and Nelson Ashby,
whose love, guidance, support and
life example have been an inspiration
to me throughout life.

of my husband
Brent A. Boyink
whose faith set an example for our family,
whose love surrounded us, and
whose teaching was to face life
through bending with the changes
it brought, not breaking.

Betty Boyink Publishing theme quilt pattern books are:

Baskets for Quilters
Child's Play for Quilters
Creating Memory Quilts
Christmas for Quilters
Double Wedding Ring Design Variations
Fans Galore for Modern Quilters
Flower Gardens & Hexagons
Michigan Quilters & Their Designs
Nautical Voyages for Quilters
Nine Patch Design Adventures
Quilt Challenges
Quilters Hearts w/Flowing Ribbons
Star Quest for Quilters
Trees & Leaves for Quilters

Other products include:
12 & 18-inch Graph Paper tablets
Plastic templates

Please send self addressed stamped envelope for product information.

About the Author

Betty Boyink began quilting in the early 1970's experimenting with design, color and fabric coming together. Her artist's palette is a stash of material labeled "blues", "reds", and all colors of the rainbow. Her quilt designs, based on tradition, are updated for today's look. She often has many quilts at various stages.

Betty became known nationally when she was invited to present President Gerald Ford a bicentennial quilt in the oval office of the White House. The Smithsonian Institute, Washington, DC, requested her bicentennial evening skirt in 1976 for its collection.

Betty is a National Quilting Association Certified Teacher, teaching all across the US, Canada and Europe. She has annually organized the North Woods Quilting Retreat since 1981. Betty is one of the coordinators of the Hoffman Fabric Challenge, now in its ninth year. She and Brent organized the 1990 national US Coast Guard 200th Anniversary quilt show. The Holland, Michigan Tulip Festival invited her to present a one woman show in 1992 with over 100 of her quilts being shown.

Student needs for patterns for projects led to research into our rich heritage of traditional quilt patterns. Several quilts pictured in this book use these patterns.

Tablets of 12 and 18-inch graph paper were added to the product line in the early 1980's. Plastic templates of favorite patterns from the books, including attic windows, were produced to speed the process of quiltmaking.

Betty has been trained for Stephens Ministries.

Introduction

The art of creative design used in the making of quilts has helped express feelings. Fabrics and textiles are meant to be touched. Most people find it impossible to walk through a clothing store or fabric shop without "feeling" the fabrics.

Fabrics are like comfort foods. They trigger memories. They provoke dreams. The soft touch of flannel consoles a youngster. Taffeta excites a teen trying on that prom gown. Satin speaks thoughts of love for the bride. Wool brings warm thoughts. Silk expresses grandeur. And so it is with the many textured fabrics we touch through life.

When fabrics are combined to make quilts they become the quiltmakers medium for expressing joy, sorrow, happiness, sadness, patriotism and an array of other emotions. Those who see the finished quilt may share the emotions of the maker or their emotional response may be entirely different. The source of fabrics can evoke memories or the quilt pattern may remind us of a story from the past.

Quilts reach out to the sense of touch and warm us from the icy cold of the weather when used as bed coverings. More importantly, they can bring a warmth to the soul. Often their creative beauty warms the heart. The source of the fabric can be the important memory, or the pattern name may tell us the story.

Life experiences are relayed in many different folk art forms. For example, the Ukrainian painted eggs help pass the Easter story from one generation to the next as the eggs tell the familiar Biblical stories. Probably no folk art form is more powerful than the combination of the sense of touch with the artistic beauty of quilts.

Through the making of quilts and the stories quilts tell, my hope is that those who are hurting from losses they have experienced will find comfort in the pages of this book. May it inspire your creative outlet for expressing feelings. Creatively dealing with the challenge does not make it go away, but does provide a means of working through grief, frustrations and some of the problems found in the living of life.

This work is written primarily in short, direct sentences using a conversational style. Many adjectives or descriptive phrases have been eliminated. This was done for two reasons. First, a person going through the stages of loss often has a short attention span. The power of concentration is not there. Second, the need persisted to communicate as much helpful information as possible to today's busy people. There is just not enough time!

Reading is encouraged; some books I have found helpful are listed in the References. But more and more we are a visual and touch oriented, sensual society. Making a quilt may be part of a solution to allow us to look out the attic window to a brighter tomorrow.

It is with gratitude that this manuscript has come to the printed word stage. A composite of stories are told so we may share how to creatively work through some of the changes that occur in life. Review the chapter titles to begin reading where your interest lies.

Acknowledgments

A very special thank you goes to my daughters and their husbands, Beverly and Jeffrey, Barbara and Charlie, and Beth Amanda. Beverly, the social worker of the family, has added her wisdom gained from education and practical experience in the field. Her husband Jeffrey, a United Methodist minister, has brought the spiritual strength. Their professional training and willingness to share their expertise make this more than a personal story of a quilt maker using the tools of her trade to cope with the changes life has brought.

And a thank you goes to the extended family for their nurturing care.

Thank you to quilters all across the country who have shared a caring spirit. A special thanks to Peggy and Holice Turnbow. Thank you to the many wonderful people who provided Hospice care both in Virginia and Michigan, particularly Jane Thomson and Andrea Harris.

Finally, thanks go to Reverand Charles F. Garrod, Carter Houck, and Donna O'Toole for their comments and suggestions.

Table of Contents

Chapter 1. My Story 10-18
Chapter 2. Loss 20-29
Chapter 3. Feelings 32-38
Chapter 4. A Need to Say Goodbye 40-43
Chapter 5. Life in the Real World 46-55
Chapter 6. HELP! Where are the Words? 58-66
Chapter 7. Return to Creative Life 67-81
Chapter 8. Piecing My Life Together 84-85
Bibliographical References 86-87
Your Notes, My Notes 88

Artwork and/or Patterns:
    Pattern for Attic Windows 18-19
    Crazy Patch, Flower Garden 30-31
    Quilt Blocks 38-39
    Dogwood 44-45
    Jacob's Ladder 66
    Guiding Star pattern 81-83

Quilt Photographs:
    Attic Windows . . . . (jacket cover)
    Celebration of Life 48-49
    Stars & Stripes, Discovering World Peace 52-53
    Slip Through the Cracks, Drunkard's Path 56-57
    Morning Glory Fan; Memorial, Bow Tie 60-61
    The Star Oak, Autumn Star 64-65
    Trip Around World, Ballerina Recital 68-69
    Country Roads to City Streets, Dogwood 72-73
    Paths of Wedded Love, Home and Heart 76-77
    Guiding Star Cross 80

Chapter 1
MY STORY

It is with great trepidation that the words begin to flow. For you see, I am a very private person and not accustomed to sharing my innermost thoughts. Imagine the shock when a friend comforted me a few days after my husband's sudden death by saying she hoped I would do something creative with what had happened. This was the first of many such nudges that kept playing a theme in the mind while the heart began to heal.

The momentum of ideas and material was like a snowball rolling down hill getting larger and larger as it went. When information was needed, it appeared in some form; shared experiences of friends and quilters broadened out my background. Reading and research helped answer some questions, other questions remain unanswered. The tapestry of life was being woven by all these experiences with God's guidance so that they might be shared in this form.

I hope that through the reading of my experiences, sharing the quilts, and working through loss and grief creatively, we will all grow more at peace. Yes, we do "piece" quilts together much as we often have to piece our lives together. The seams come unravelled in our stitching as fate unravels the shared dreams of relationships.

I grew up in northern Virginia with a happy childhood in a typical family with four children. After school, several years of working at the Department of State proved a valuable experience. A double "double wedding ring" ceremony united my sister and her husband, and Brent and me before family and friends. Three beautiful and healthy daughters were born.

Forty arrived! Time for a second career, or was it a third? Quilting had been taking more and more of my time. Designing special quilts for family members as well as experimenting with as many quilt designs as possible filled these days. Working with a United Methodist Church quilt group provided even more experience, because I was the one who made most of the tops for the ladies to quilt. We have made an average of four quilts per year for many years without ever repeating the same quilt design.

The revival of interest in the early 1970's in many of the indigenous American folk art forms opened the door for me to teach quiltmaking locally. Research for personal designs combined with class requests provided a wealth of opportunities to study the heritage of quiltmaking.

After designing a red, white and blue quilt in 1975, I inquired and became officially licensed to market patterns of the Bicentennial Star quilt pattern. This led to presenting a quilt based on the pattern to President Gerald Ford in the Oval Office at the White House. I feel honored to have a bicentennial skirt in the Smithsonian Museum, Washington, D.C.

In order to meet student needs, a format developed to share that research through theme pattern books. At that time, there were not very many quilt pattern books on the market. These books were marketed to quilt and stitchery shops. Brent's goal and my goal was to introduce a new theme pattern book each year. This meant making samples to illustrate the subject of the book, while concentrating on a wide variety of techniques using both pieced and appliqued designs. Something for everyone interested in the chosen subject!

A cottage industry began with support from the entire family. The girls would assemble, staple, prepare mailings and do many other tasks required to make a home business work. Brent, my life partner, was the other half of our endeavors, giving encouragement, wisdom gained in the business world, computer skills and lots of manpower. His photography skills were unsurpassed. He had a patience for perfection.

Quilt shows provided an opportunity for meeting quilters and sharing the labors of our production of books. Years followed of packing the car to drive to a quilt show site, setting up the booth, working the hours of the show, taking down the booth and driving back home. Travelling around the country to teach also allowed sharing a love of stitchery with quiltmakers.

Quilters responded to what the pattern books offered. Our dreams were coming true. With the youngest daughter off to college, it was back to the two of us working full time together on projects. There were many long hours of work over the design and production stages of the samples as well as the layout, paperwork and business. There was joy and satisfaction in doing what we both enjoyed. Life was just about perfect!

The girls were well on their way to achieving shared goals of education, careers and marriages. Our goal of passing on to our children the important ability to adapt to the changes presented by an ever changing world was being reached. Little did I realize that I would be required to make the most dramatic changes.

It was while at one such quilt show that a deep chest cold plagued Brent. The second afternoon he went back to the room exhausted for a nap. Upon returning to the room late that afternoon, I found he had died from pneumonia. We had no idea he had bacterial pneumonia or was as sick as he must have been.

In shock, I had to make arrangements long distance from out of state, as well as take care of many details of being far from home when tragedy strikes. But the most difficult part was to telephone the girls that their beloved Dad was gone. Now if there are tears on these lines, it is because they have flowed often as we have faced piecing a life together after the end of so many dreams.

Numbness, disbelief, and all the adjustments of facing so many decisions alone brought a load upon my shoulders. The girls and their husbands were constantly at my side for weeks working through some of the sudden grief. Family and friends, a deep faith and church family support were there when needed. The connectional network of quilters all across the country responded with loving notes and prayers.

A little over a week after the funeral, I left to present lectures and workshops for a quilt guild in Kansas. The contract was in place, airline tickets had been purchased and a guild was waiting for a program followed by workshops. My first thought was to cancel everything that spring. Then the reality of contracts and commitments set in.

The business we had worked so long and hard to build should continue as a tribute to Brent's dedication. One session for the Kansas guild was on "Double Wedding Ring" using the strip pieced method which I had developed. Many of the slides pierced my heart anew with the realization that the double wedding ring would take on a whole new meaning.

The first plan was to have the president explain the recent loss of Brent so that they would understand my emotional state. How could I remain in complete control for those days? The enthusiasm of the first few quilters who entered changed my thinking; why should my personal distress put a damper on their fun outing. I left three days later with only the president and my hostess knowing of my anguish. Somehow, the days after that slipped into months.

A year later, Brent's Mom had two major surgeries in just a few months. The loss of mobility and body functions caused great concern. Care was needed to allow healing time as her health slowly returned.

That same fall, I received word that my Mom had been put in the Hospice program and was not expected to live until the holidays. She loved the holidays with family gathered around, all the trimmings and fancy foods. With tender loving care and a will to share as much of life with her family as possible, my Mom died on March 7th following lingering heart disease. Time to prepare for her passing was needed by her, as well as training us for a life without one of the major family members.

Dad's cancer problem had been in remission for a couple years until the stress and grief of losing a life partner of over 55 years caused active growth to return. The cancer broke through to vital body organs. We were forewarned by the doctor as he evaluated Dad's condition that the death of a long time spouse often changes the timetable of life.

Dad passed away June 8th, just three months after Mom. The gentle, tender love of a mother and the strength and leadership of a loving father were qualities passed on to their children. Memories linger after the loss of both parents so close in time.

There were months of care giving and travel time back and forth to Virginia from my home in Michigan. Quick turn around times were required between show dates and care time. Meeting deadlines and schedules, carving in precious family time, and trying to keep a business going while preoccupied caused constant fatigue.

Also during these couple of years, a favorite uncle died suddenly from a heart attack. Another uncle went through successful heart bypass surgery. An aunt went through cancer surgery, with good news after final testing was done.

These events stacked up on our family in quick

succession. As happens in many families at a certain age, the generation ahead of us had reached advanced years with increasing health problems.

The time needed for a family to say goodbye had been granted which made the passing of loved parents easier to bear. Could it be their age too? Perhaps the timetable of a full life had been fulfilled.

There were not the questions that the sudden, unexpected death brings to mind, such as with my husband Brent. Why? Fifty-three is too young to die! Besides the cause of death was in most cases a curable disease...pneumonia. How could this happen? Sometimes it is not ours to know the answers.

There are times in our lives when life as we know it appears to come apart at the seams. No pun intended! Often times, we in the middle generation are faced with problems of growing children or young adults, yet are needed by elderly parents as they require more care.

Through these months of struggle, there have been joys as well. A new granddaughter arrived bringing a renewal of life and a bright ray of sunshine. Our youngest daughter Beth graduated from college and moved out into the world. But did it have to be all the way to California?

Getting away from it all to quilting events with caring friends has provided a safety valve the past many months. Through some difficult times, the universal language of love helped breathe hope through to a bleeding heart.

For the most part, I can be optimistic. But there are times when the memory of something or a spoken word can undo some of the healing that has occurred. The pain and grief overwhelm me again. It is time to struggle back once more.

Little creative time has been available for designing and making wonderful quilt patterns. There has been so much to learn and deal with that has taken time away from creative goals. A theme pattern book is at various stages of the process just waiting for completion. Fabrics have been pulled together in color groupings for projects...time just to look at them. While working on pieces, awareness of events can be worked through, faced or maybe just accepted. Creativity is explored in the chapters ahead.

The story of getting to this spot in life has been told in the first person of "I". I hope this will help you understand and move forward with me through parts of life where great losses have occurred. We shall switch to a different style of writing by moving from my personal story to a composite of comments and research that express the desired message.

In this way, the full meaning will be maintained while avoiding any possibility of causing pain to family, friends or other folks who have shared their stories along life's way. In my case, the losses have been death, yet many of the shared comments are the result of other types of loss explored in Chapter 2. We will keep some of the personal touch with the writing by identifying individuals with names chosen randomly.

By sharing a part of my life with you through the written word as well as comments of others and research,

I hope you will come to understand the importance creativity can have in helping one rebuild. Creativity for you may be music, art, cooking, building or woodworking, decorating, or another activity.

Many of the pictured quilts illustrated have full size patterns in one of the series of theme pattern books. The quilt photographs help guide us through some of the creative approaches to life I have experimented with over the years.

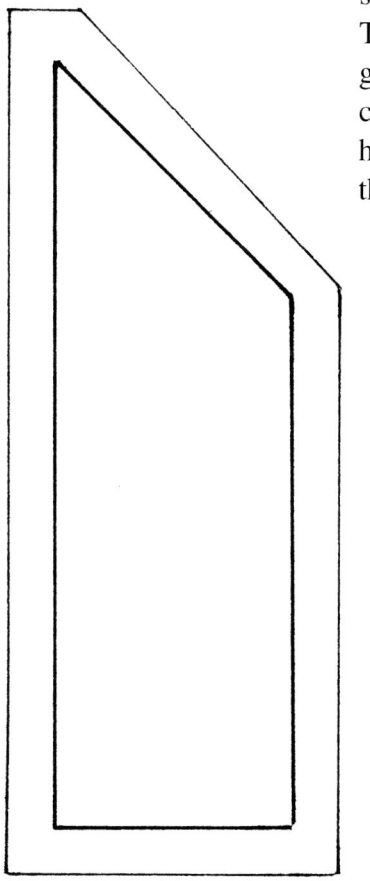

Piece dark side to square, add light window sill.

Piece in rows, sashing strips optional.

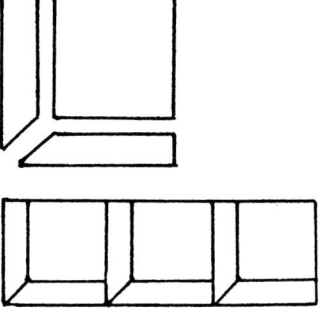

Attic Window

Jacket cover quilt, illustration on title page
4-inch block, 33 x 64-inches, 1/2-inch sashing

Depth of design has been increasingly explored by artists from all venues. One such design quilters have taken to all lengths is called attic windows, the quilt design on the jacket cover. Sashing strips further the illusion of depth. Changing colors in these strips as well as the border maintain the light and dark areas.

Use the window pattern idea to portray what you might see looking out a window. Choose fabrics to interpret this idea. Is your view of trees? Skyscrapers? Or possibly a garden of flowers with sky colors towards top. Piece your dreams! See my notes on page 88.

Actual pattern line is darker, with 1/4-inch seam allowance the finer line. Window sill and side of window are same template. To piece, add sill and side to the square shape. Blocks may be set together or add sashing. Assemble in rows and add border. Add quilt batting and backing fabric. Photo to check depth. Quilt and bind off.

Chapter 2
Loss

Life used to be simple. Family ties were strong and they lived close together which allowed loss to be learned, dealt with and worked through. Extended families are less common now. With the mobility of the modern age, we often face loss without that support network to cushion the painful experience. Learning to deal creatively with problems to maintain a balanced mental state becomes an important factor. We will look at loss with real life experiences through a composite of stories. Random names have been chosen.

Loss occurs any time there is a change in what is familiar. Webster's dictionary defines loss as "1, failure to hold, keep, or preserve; 2, that which is lost; 3, wastage; 4, defeat, ruin." 'At a loss' is bewildered, uncertain." These are powerful words that describe many of the feelings associated with a loss.

Loss is the event and grief is the emotional response, or the process of dealing with loss. Loss may be of persons, objects or security or a combination of these. We can distance ourselves from facing the loss, or "feeling the pain" as it may be stated. Reality usually forces the issue.

Often the "process" of grief has been neatly put into descriptive words that relay steps. These steps can be helpful to identify feelings and why we react to circumstances as we do. Different sources have various identifying labels necessary to re-establish our equilibrium after a loss. In his book *Grief Counseling & Grief Therapy*, J. William Worden lists four basic tasks to aid in "grief work" as it is called. The required work takes time and an amazing amount of energy.

1. Accept the reality of loss. Accepting the loss takes time to intellectually face the fact of the absence. The finality of the loss usually comes before the emotions will accept it.
2. The pain of grief needs to be worked through. It is actual physical pain as well as emotional pain. Pain may be prolonged or avoided by drugs, alcohol, denial, travel to run away from it or changing the thought process. Try to feel the pain and know that someday it will lessen.
3. Adjustment to a world without the individual. Skills need to be developed to cope with all aspects of life. Many are not recognized until time brings us face to face with the reality of the questions that need answers. Growth occurs as these skills become routine tasks.
4. Emotionally relocate the loss to move on with life. Find a place to locate the loss in emotional life that allows moving forward to face life. Remember the lost one, but holding on to the past should not keep one from living today.

From a lay person's perspective, we could condense the above four stages to shock, pain, adjustment and find a way to continue living. Shock temporarily provides an anesthetic for sorrow we are unable to accept. The pain is very real and often shows physical symptoms. The complexity of relationships and types of loss enter the scene as we try to cope with the adjustments. The emotions of anger, guilt, and resentment all play out their rolls.

Depression, loneliness and panic settle in as days, weeks, and months stretch out. This is the reason I have started sending a "thinking of you" card or written note a month or two after a loss. The full realization of the loss settles in with the passing of time. Notes are important.

Gradually hope returns as we go through the stages of grief (not around, not under, not over, or any other shortcut but "through" the stage door). Time and a support network help as you work toward healing. With healing, one realizes you never get over the loss, just learn to accept the changes and continue living. We are individuals carrying bits and pieces of all that has touched our lives.

Talking with someone who has faced similar circumstances is comforting and helpful. Support therapy provides some good benefits whether it is with a professional or a knowledgeable friend. For example, Chris could talk with her weekly quilting group because others in the group could identify with what she was saying. She felt these caring friends saved her a counseling bill. Do you have a support group or compassionate and caring person to talk over problems? Or a professional counselor?

We begin facing losses from our infancy. A new

mother leaves Annie to go to work. Remember when six year old Cindy was so upset with the loss of that front tooth. A beloved pet dog dies. The teen years bring rapid change with personality growth, jobs and job losses, girl friend or boy friend issues which may cause loss, athletic losses, and many others. For some, leaving home for college means the loss of security and known boundaries. Others have a different feeling! Leaving the family for married life also has mixed blessings that may include loss. Over spenders face the loss of credit cards.

Strong, often conflicting, emotions are experienced as children leave home. Each child in a family is important and leaves a nostalgic sadness in the hearts of those left. In most cases the last one to leave affects parents the most. The emptiness is emphasized when the child was a busy one with lots of activities and friends. Another factor is the distance away from home and the possibility of visits. On the other hand, some parents count their blessings when children leave.

Clara noticed a distancing of her daughter from family activities after she left home. It took time, courage and nerve for Brenda to come out to announce to her parents that she was a Lesbian. In the 1980's and 1990's, there is a whole new change in lifestyle with more openness about sexual orientation. It was a shock to her parents, who asked "where did we go wrong?" By educating each other, they could begin to rebuild their relationship and work through to a better understanding.

It takes time for families to accept the changes brought about by a chosen life style different from their own. Other family members need to be included in discussions for family unity. It was not easy, but the wish for happiness and acceptance brought Clara's daughter back in this family's case.

A job loss is one that has all kinds of repercussions. In horse racing, it is advised to accept your losses as quickly as possible in order to move on with the next phase. The next phase is the yearling in the corral waiting to be broken for the start of a new racing career. Not many jobs are quite the game of chance that this example is, but in the business world we can understand the importance of making decisions to minimize loss. That is, until it affects us individually.

Unfortunately the job market is often the employer's game with just about as little human kindness or lack of feeling as stated above. In many areas the labor market is infused with insecurity and apprehension. The loss of a job affects most of life, especially the person's self esteem. Family and community relationships are affected. Besides it plays havoc with the family budget!

Relocation due to job changes means loss of familiar surroundings, friendships and school changes. It can separate the family temporarily until details of the move are worked out. Sometimes the separation is more permanent when children are left behind because of latter years of school or early jobs. What happens when the other half of the couple has a job that does not move? This has elements of becoming a bigger loss.

Retirement from one's chosen field is a very exciting time for many people. For others, it produces anxiety.

Sally puts it like it is for some, "I married him for better or worse, but not for lunch." Is she saying there is a need for space, or make your own peanut butter sandwich?

Retirement for Arthur meant no more contact with coworkers who had become friends, no more secretary to take care of the details and feeling he was not needed. Recognition, acceptance and belonging; three areas important to make life meaningful, are being tampered with. Adjustment will take time. If this is your time in life, be sure to read Chapter 7 for some creative ideas.

The big "C" word from years past; cancer is still frightening for most of us. Even though we are more open in discussing this disease and more information about it is available, people often experience losses beginning at the time of diagnosis. Physical abilities, positive body image, and a sense of immortality are but a few. For some, anger and denial are less healthy ways to handle the news of cancer. After the initial shock, education takes over for others as they learn as much as possible about the disease from a health perspective.

It has been proven that attitude plays an important part in the treatment of cancer patients. Samantha calmly commented as she shared about her mother, "after all she lived with cancer for over 40 years." Notice the word was "lived" with and not coped with, tolerated, or fought. Maybe one of the reasons for the years adding up is the creative ways one learns to "live" with the disease.

Statistically, one woman in eight will have breast cancer. We hear mammogram, yearly check-up, and yet still put it off because we are not one of the statistics. Are we immune? Winifred shared that the loss of her breast caused physical, emotional and cosmetic adjustments to get through. It was frightening! The changes in appearance affects self-image, but life does go forward. Expressing the questions and concerns with doctors, family and friends was an important emotional medicine. Sharing experiences by talking and listening to others in a support group was therapeutic and essential for her.

Aging process losses have been greatly minimized with the miracles of modern medicine. A quilter friend visiting while at a quilt show relayed the health problems and frustrations at the limitations she had experienced the last few months. Christine commented after she left, "Getting old isn't for sissies." Nurture yourself with kindness and tender loving care so that you can share a love of life for as long as possible. And may your friends continue to provide nurturing care even when your routine of life is changed due to illness.

The loss of a loved one in death may be the greatest loss one faces. We must each face it whether we are prepared or not. Grandparents often prepare the way by their courageous early words of comfort. We may have heard "Do not grieve for me for I've had a good life." Often parents and that generation are ready to be free of the cares of life here on earth.

There can be a rude awakening when suddenly there is a change in the generation progression. It is said that the greatest loss is the loss of a child, whether an infant or an adult child. Three important sustaining factors when we are faced with the grief death brings appear to be faith, family and friends. We can depend on them.

The loss of a life partner through death causes deep anguish. The hurt is so painful and deep, you may feel no one has ever experienced such sorrow. It can be a struggle to make it one hour at a time, or day by day.

Adjustments begin with one of the biggest learning curves most individuals will ever face. The stark realty of the changes begins to sink in shortly after the hectic funeral days. Keeping busy and being allowed time to grieve, one gradually begins to chart a new course with goals for living.

After healing time has passed from the death, a closure of this phase of life is possible because the individual simply is gone. But memories are often jolted from the past to the present by a current situation. We walk today carrying the past as we move forward to the future. We could look at the stages of life not as a beginning nor an ending, but as a continuing journey.

If divorce is the reason for a loss, the association often continues making it difficult to work completely through the loss at that time. A similar learning curve to the one referred to above begins as a life alone begins to take shape.

In divorce, stress most likely builds up over a period of time causing many complex issues which need to be resolved. When the partners are mismatched, loss diminishes quickly after the stress of the divorce is past. The complexity of parent/child relationships adds to the stress, relocation of one of the parties is needed, and dividing the accumulated treasures and junk are just the tip of the iceberg of issues that need solutions. A decision to allow time, patience, and empathy for all involved helps the family move toward peace.

Nannette loved to cook; she gained 10 pounds a month the first three months after Allen passed away. Food had become her way of being creative, keeping busy and providing comfort. However, this was detrimental to her diabetic health problem. Her diabetic system needed special attention. Be tuned in to your body's needs and take care of your health.

If the lilies in the field are cared for, then surely one must feel the security of knowing that there is care for us also. When we can begin to accept the change that has occurred, we can move toward finding inner peace. We cannot relive the past, bring the past back, or redo any of the yesterdays. If we dwell on what we have lost or been denied, we may overlook the beauty of the lily.

When we can identify the blessings that have been provided for us today, we can appreciate the good life has to offer, and offer praise for the hope of tomorrow. "I have learned to be content with whatever I have. . . I can do everything through him who gives me strength." Philippians 4:11, 13 (NIV) On most days I have the hope of tomorrow, but there are times of deeply feeling the loss of loved ones.

Use a creative approach to occupy yourself with what is familiar so that your mind is free to wander and work through some of the feelings. An example might be the cutting of strips for a quilt top; one that does not take much thought. It is not the time for a Baltimore type of applique quilt, which is considered the ultimate in the quilt world. Too difficult, tedious, and time consuming!

Keep your work super simple during these days when the mind is off thinking about other things. Running that sewing machine can be therapeutic if it is mindless routine. Watch for the 1/4-inch seam allowance but let your thoughts wander. Build something with your hands, remodel, or decorate a room. Find your interests, then find a task that leaves your mind free to roam as you create something.

Allow time for processing what is happening. It is healthier and aids in healing.

Grandmother's Flower Garden

Grandmother's Flower Garden is made of perfectly shaped hexagon pieces going together to form the design. It is one of the most recognized patterns from our rich heritage in quiltmaking. Hexagon shape scraps were sewn together to make something beautiful from the remnants of sewing.

A number of factors help the remnants of our lives go together after experiencing loss.

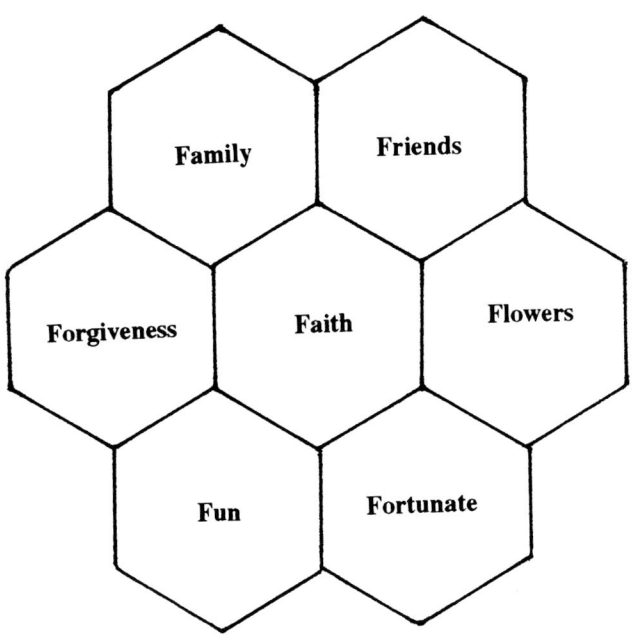

Crazy Patch

The Crazy Patch type of quilt is made of irregular shapes put together. Sometimes life appears a bit on the crazy side, but we should remember the beauty of the completed whole.

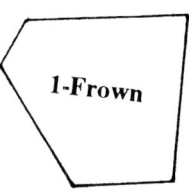
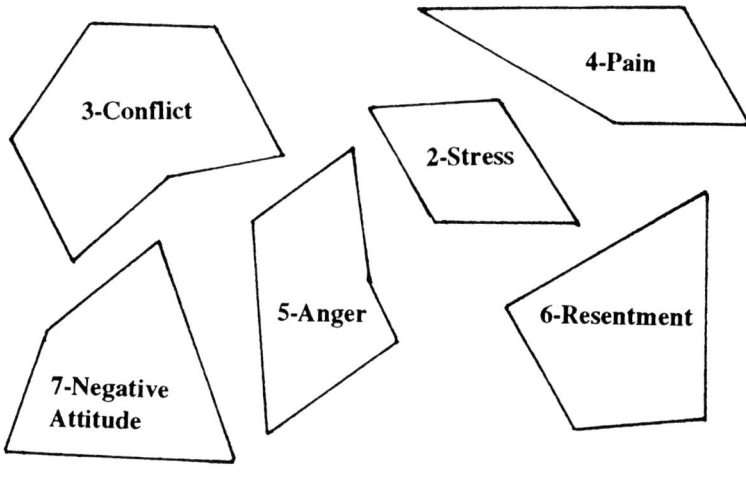

Chapter 3
Feelings

Feelings are the way we react to what is happening to us at that time. Feelings run the spectrum from as simple as sad or happy to despondent or elated. Some words that relay good feelings might be excited, surprised, satisfied, appreciative, affectionate, relieved, and calm. The content of happy could range from cheerful to exuberant.

Some feelings that go along with sad might be described as distressed, frightened, anxious, angry, disgusted, ashamed or embarrassed. The intensity of sad might go all the way from gloomy to devastated.

By thinking of a descriptive word to associate with feelings, it helps us identify our feelings. When we understand what our feelings are, it may ease our mind to know our feelings are within the normal range given the problems we are facing at that time. They often come in a mixed bag! Perhaps that is where the comment comes from, "every cloud has a silver lining to be found."

Finding a way to express feelings may help bring healing to the troubled. Once an emotion is expressed, whether verbally, in writing or through some creative outlet, it is less intense. The emotions of one who has faced loss can often be read in the facial expression or the tone of the voice. Just as sad emotions are readable, our body language also relays the joys of life when they come our way. We express both joy and sadness through tears.

It is okay to cry; let the tears flow! Or, do we become

stoic keeping our emotions inside? Tears speak of a love that was important enough to feel deeply. Tears honor a loved one's life and contribution. It has been reported that emotional stress builds up harmful chemicals that can be released with tears. People who cry are healthier and suffer less from stress related ailments.

Be aware of high stress times. By identifying stress, we just may be taking the first step toward developing a routine to cope. Some stress might be associated with certain individuals, some with a location, some with situations, and others you may name that are particular to you. We can often avoid or prepare ahead of time for the emotional surge that occurs with stress. The build up of one stressful event after another creates pressure until all it takes is a simple comment or memory to break the dam of stored up feelings.

When Cheryl felt the tears welling up, she consciously allowed herself to cry three tissues worth. After that she would physically move to a different room, read, take a walk or do a task that required concentration. Start a new project! Make this activity busy work that keeps the mind free to process the reasons for the painful release of emotions. Most of the time, a physical relocation or activity helped ease the pain of the moment. Cheryl did confess that occasionally she dried a tissue to hold more tears by waving it in midair. After time and healing, tears and emotions become more controllable.

Finding the place to allow feelings to happen is important. Notice a child arriving home after he has had a disappointment...there is the safety in releasing pent up emotion in loving, comfortable surroundings. A comfortable chair can be set up with a few easy reading books and a box of tissues handy. The reading books should vary from therapeutic or healing, to light and uplifting. Of course include your favorite quilt idea book to dream over.

Ruth lost her 39 year old son from a sudden heart attack. She found the saltiness of the tears were not as noticeable when water washed away the tear drops during showers. Showers became an emotional cleansing time.

An automobile ride can be a time away from the world. You can think while driving out in the country or down the freeway, but not in busy city traffic. No one hears if you talk right out loud. Watch your speed...or you may go as fast as your feelings are running! Seventy, eighty, ninety; it is easier to understand some of the catastrophic accidents that have occurred with stressed individuals once you have driven in their tracks. You are in the right setting with well chosen routes to begin healing and enjoy some of the beauty of the world.

A brisk walk or physical activity can also work as a release to emotional stress. Toward the end of the walk, slow down to take time to enjoy nature's bounty for a lift to the spirit. There comes a time when tears or feelings are stored deeper in the well as healing takes place.

Choosing to stop the tears to continue living may help avoid depression that continued crying can cause. Besides, the head and nose fill up adding discomfort and more tension to what is already happening. There are times we feel some of the symptoms of depression because of the difficulties of life. These are temporary, and gradually ease as we work toward solving the problems that have brought about the changes. Check for signs that alert you to more serious conditions that might need attention.

Signs of depression are: 1-disturbance in sleep (too much or too little); 2-disturbance in appetite (too much or too little); 3-moods of feeling sad, weepy, angry or irritable; 4-lack of motivation; 5-change in functioning such as in daily activities of personal hygiene and/or home care; 6-decrease in or lack of concentration; 7-thoughts of suicide or wanting to hurt yourself (indicates more severe depression).

Professionals call it clinical depression if three or more of the listed conditions exist. Doctor ordered medication can improve symptoms when a bio-chemical imbalance has caused the depression. Counseling may be called for if signs of depression are evident.

Ever feel the tears just below the surface in yourself, held so tightly in check like a bottle ready to pop its cork? Once the cork is released, the fizz releases excess air. There is not a return to normal (before the fermentation), but a new and very different tasting beverage has evolved. Tears can be a similar release for us as we face overwhelming problems. Life does not return to what it once was before the loss, but becomes new and different.

A goal might be to work toward finding pleasure in the life you have built after a loss. Notice the word "built" was used, for that fits the task at hand. A strong foundation is built from the bottom up or inside out. This sounds easy in words, but often life situations come with lots of complications.

One such complication might be guilt feelings, which need to be dealt with carefully. Guilt feelings are often related to regrets. A few are very real experiences while others are regrets weighing us down unnecessarily. The weight of guilt may cause a lack of self confidence. Gaining self confidence in new situations gives one a better chance for good feelings. Learning to accept our imperfections, forgiving ourselves and those who have hurt us are steps toward healing.

Hugs can be wonderful healing for some, while others feel threatened with the closeness. Imagine a circle around you as a comfortable zone. If another individual approaches too close, there can be a breakdown of communication. Emotional upheaval brings change that may cause a different response. A return to your normal comfort zone should occur after some healing time if you were a hugger before the loss.

Remember in the Introduction there was a statement made that said we were "more and more a visual and touch oriented sensual society." Human need for feeling the touch of others through hugging is being recognized from songs to art, from infants to the elderly, and beyond. Author Virginia Satir put it this way: "We need 4 hugs a day for survival. We need 8 hugs a day for maintenance. We need 12 hugs a day for growth." Giving a hug doesn't take a battery or electric power, but it is as powerful as a smile to light up another person's day.

If hugs are not for you, find a way to protect yourself

from the invasion of closeness. Extend a hand in greeting. Learning to read the comfort zone when comforting another person may improve the relationship.

You have to feel the pain to find hope and joy in life. Linda was taken aback the first time she laughed out loud after an upsetting event in her life. Was she not miserable? The release of tears quickly followed. But for that moment, there was a spark of hope that someday life could be happy again. If not happy, she was heading in the right direction with the sound of laughter. It is okay to laugh while grieving.

When in crisis, your sense of humor may leave you. The ability to look at life with a sense of humor may be the buoy that guides us out of dangerous waters. It is a valuable asset.

Taking care of oneself is essential in the healing process. The physical needs of rest, proper nutrition, and exercise are often the easy ones. Play just for the fun of it is an idea that many workaholics have difficulty with. Good emotional health may take more work. Confidence in who we are, liking ourselves, and a good attitude make us more in harmony.

Alex worked in a difficult situation which caused much stress buildup. He used to say to himself "attitude adjustment time" when he felt himself slipping into a negative mode. It helped to identify that even though he was not the problem, his response and attitude could help defuse the difficult situation.

Life is easier when we learn to trust the safety of floating on the water rather than fighting the waves and sinking with fear.

We may have read where quilts could tell stories of our lives if they could speak. Feelings are an important part of those stories. It is possible to work through feelings while making a quilt that relates to the situation. Political statements were made in early times by the name given a quilt block design. More recently, there is a well known divorce quilt that has appeared at shows and in publications.

One quilter used the same pieced block to make a series of four blocks to help her face and work through the disease and death of a grandchild. Through the use of color and a touch of applique, she portrayed the shock of learning of the disease in the first one, the pain and feelings of helplessness during the stages, the finality of the actual loss, and an acceptance after time allowed for those feelings.

Traditional names given quilt blocks speak of feelings. One that comes to mind immediately that speaks volumes is Crosses and Losses. For more names and designs to ponder for a project, note the names of the blocks listed as well as some of the quilt designs pictured.

Carpenters Wheel, also called Dutch Rose, from Star Quest for Quilters

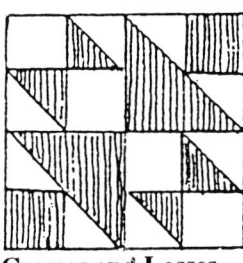

Crosses and Losses

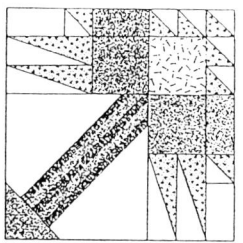

**Tree of Life, from
Trees & Leaves for Quilters**

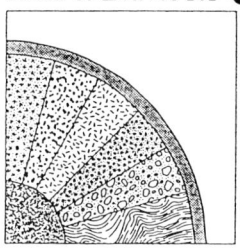

**Grandmother's Fan, see page 60
Fans Galore for Modern Quilters**

**Drunkard's Path, see page 57
from Curve Template**

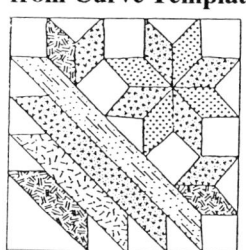

**Friendship Basket
from Baskets for Quilters**

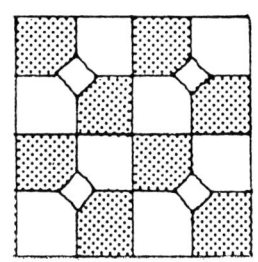

Bow Tie, see page 61

Love Entangled

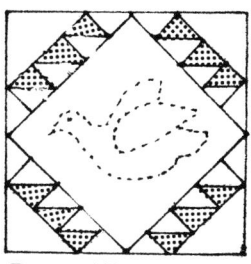

Dove of Peace

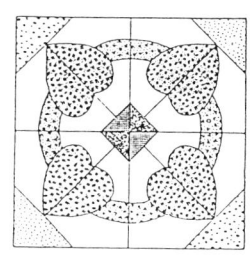

**Hearts and Rings
from Quilters Hearts**

39

Chapter 4
A Need to Say Goodbye

Do we look in a window or look out toward the world? In quilting, there is a block that has a center square, bordered on the bottom with a light window seal effect, and on the left side with a dark shadow of the side frame. The dark and light provide the perception of depth in this Attic Window design which may be seen on the jacket cover. Sometimes it is hard to see beyond the reflection of the past, but a scene is out there to be viewed from the perspective of the attic window above.

A relationship begins with a hello, maybe eye contact, or some other form of greeting. There are the minutes, hours, days, weeks, months or years that are shared, some more intimately than others. Maybe the relationship is between a parent and child. Does there need to be a goodbye at the end of the time together? Many physiologists feel that a closure or understanding of goodbye is essential to good mental health.

For people that have the opportunity to say goodbye to loved ones, there appears to be an easier, more bearable grief period. Most often, a sudden death or loss does not allow such time. Our natural inclination is the reluctance to accept the inevitable. Avoiding reality is a protective measure until the shock can be absorbed more gradually.

Death is such a final goodbye that the heart refuses to respond to what the head is telling it. This is often seen in cases of terminal illness. The time spent in caring for the individual often works as a preparatory time.

Individuals that have shared so intimate a part of life will always be a part of us and our memories. A goodbye doesn't make those years any less important. Think of it as a way that we face reality and continue to live, without the daily contact with the other individual. Do keep in mind that it may be much easier for the head to read, understand and see the importance of these thoughts. The emotions of the heart often cannot face the reality!

How can there be a good-bye in divorce situations when there has to be constant interaction when children are involved? While the details of a divorce settlement are being worked out, a different relationship needs to begin. The relationship can continue down the path of the marriage or start to take the road toward its end. The acceptance of the end of the marital bond brings healing to the broken hearted.

The healing goodbye of the marital relationship allows one to move forward to rebuild a life. For divorcing parents, an open line of communication has to continue for the best interests of the children.

Bonita mentioned that the goodbye felt completed when she had her diamonds reset into a very different type of ring she called her "divorce ring". Rings are a very strong emotional statement from the joyous receiving to either removal or restyling. If life were perfect the rings would be passed to the next generation. Is that seeing through a rose colored attic window in today's world of divorce?

Sometime after the healing process, there may appear on the scene another friend or soul mate. This can be difficult for children of whatever age to understand, deal with, or accept. Talk about accepting this new individual into the family circle brings out the guard! It could be that there is a need to maintain the family unit as it was, even though there is an empty spot. Make sure there is an understanding this is not a replacement but a decision to continue to live. It is hard to remember that changes have occurred and continue to evolve.

The natural progression of parents moving toward the end of life surely is a goodbye that affects us in many ways. Long into a terminal illness, a mother asks her care giver children if they "are ready to let her go to heaven." In other words, she is saying it is time for her to die, but is aware that maybe those around her are just not yet prepared to "let her go" or to say goodbye.

Or, a father will indicate that there are things left unsaid that need to be said before his heart can be at peace to face death. The answer to either situation can be a soul searching one trying to read the correct message into the comment. Is it a time for reassuring of the importance of living? Or, is it a time to accept the reality of what is being asked? Not easy! The questions need our compassion.

Another example is Marlene. She was brought back to life after surgery when she thought she had already died. She was angry with the doctor, even more angry with her children as the slow recovery period turned into weeks and months. The situation was nearly unbearable for both mother and adult children. A talk one day revealed the children felt they had not been prepared to let her go.

The gradual process for Marlene was to begin cutting the apron strings and moving more out of the daily routine for both mother and children. Her daughter commented that if mother had another illness, she felt the time would have been allowed to work through the natural progression of preparation for leaving this world.

The view out the window or the view in the window of our lives changes according to the events that take place. For many, some days it is hard to see beyond the reflection of the past, but a scene is out there gradually developing that is right for each person. The new scene building needs our full attention and nurturing care as we say goodbye to part of the past.

Dogwood

The dogwood is the state flower for Virginia and North Carolina. A beautiful flower with four petals, dogwood blossoms have a brown spot or tear at the outer edge of the petal. Is this tear or spot symbolic of the loss of perfection?

The door of healing from emotional stress, physical ailments, spiritual withdrawal, and mental anguish opens wider as the whole person heals. Time is required for the healing process. The experiences we go through change us, open us to be more receptive, and ultimately cause growth.

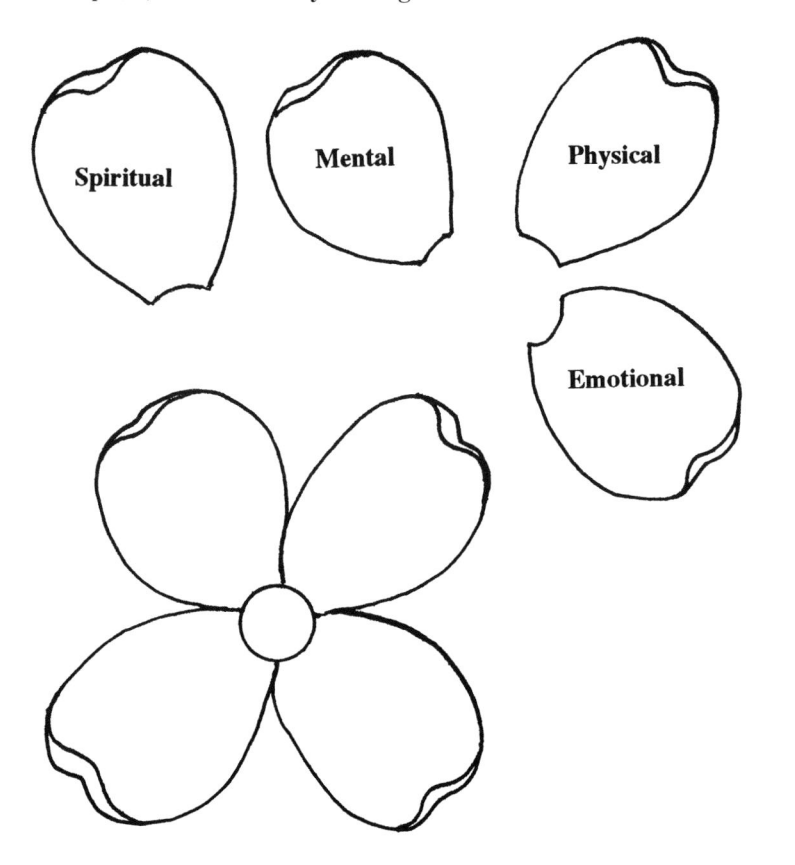

Applique

Some designs are appliqued, or fabric shapes applied on top of the background fabric to make the picture. To make, use the following drawing as your guide. Trace each shape on paper, freezer paper or template plastic. For applique, trace around actual template. Choose either a 3/8 or 1/4-inch seam allowance. Add the seam allowance as you cut out the shape. You may wish to press fabric over a freezer paper pattern for exact size. Position on background, stitch in place with a blind applique stitch. Embroider the line that makes the turned back brown spot for a more realistic look. Applique the stem first. Two dogwood leaves are positioned opposite each other along the stem.

Chapter 5
Life in the Real World

Unfortunately life is not the "pollyanna" picture of the live-happily-ever-after scenario of the perfect family. It would be wonderful if it were. Take a look at the following stories relaying events of life in the real world. If we do everything in our power from that small place we inhabit to make this a better world for those around us, the side effects will be a happier world for us too. It will not be an easy task, but understanding others as they carry their burdens is a good beginning.

You may recognize yourself in one of the stories, or disagree with one of the characters, want to stand up for the injustices or applaud the turn of events. Hopefully we will observe relationships and the interaction of our daily contacts with other people.

Ginny received a telephone call from an investment broker salesman with a recognized firm, asking for the man of the home by name. When told that he was no longer there, the salesman rudely hastened to end the telephone call. This left Ginny feeling that she wasn't important, with no money sense, and furious that the world now treated her like a second class citizen.

Wasn't it only a few months before that she was respected as the "lady of the house"? Wouldn't you like to see Ginny telephone the salesman back to ask the name of his competitor...she had a million to invest!

A simple acknowledgment that his firm stood ready

to help her with financial problems or investments would have changed the scenario. This action would have left her with dignity all people deserve and possibly gained him a new customer.

Speaking of finances, that is an area where there can be problems if managing the family finances is a new experience. Think of a home with a paycheck as funds received, expenses paid out, interest expenses with in-the-red books or investments with excess funds. That is what a Home Management 101 course would teach, however most learn family finances on the job.

Often one individual handles the finances for the family. This leaves the other one at a vulnerable disadvantage if suddenly he or she is thrust into the position of handling the finances.

Sharing family financial responsibilities from time to time would help tune in to current trends in the budget. Discussing decisions on finances at important junctions avoids disappointments and hurt on down the road. Unnecessary stress can be avoided if the whole job of family finances should be on your shoulders by the loss of the entrusted individual. Just as a project pattern or knowledgeable friend helps with our stitchery problems, trusted companies or an expert can help if finances are unknown areas. Selected reading material can be helpful.

Sam had asked his dad to write down on paper the basic facts that would be needed to take care of immediate needs should something happen to his dad. Dad kept putting it off feeling it was a nuisance and there would be time next week. A sudden stroke left Dad a

Continued page 50

Celebration of Life quilt, 44 x 54-inches

Shapes have always intrigued me, particularly the hexagon. This shape appears as through it were a stretched out hexagon. You may have seen the shape in tile flooring.

The one patch white work quilt pictured on the opposite page was made as a family piece. The dove, symbol of the holy spirit, is appliqued on one corner to be used at a baptismal service for a new granddaughter. White has been used as a baptismal color for centuries. Subtle shading of different white print fabrics creates an overall design.

Quilts can be made of a single shape, or one patch. Often these were made with each fabric a different, colorful print. Possibly the name given to this one patch shape is the reason there appears to be so few quilts in existence of the pattern. Early records call it the Coffin Block because its shape resembles the mummy type of grave boxes.

It seems appropriate to honor all aspects of life from birth to death. The opposite corner has an appliqued floral arrangement when the quilt is used as a casket cover. The quilted wreath of cable and flowers in a continuous circle is representative of the whole of life.

An extended illness allowed one family to return to an age old custom of final preparation. A coffin was made of walnut wood with beautiful grain lines. Skillfully crafted by a master carpenter, the coffin was lined by other family members. Shared family experiences became cherished memories as the creative efforts came together.

Many cultures have cloths used for special times. A Christening dress or blanket, a treasured keepsake, is handed down from generation to generation. A California friend has an Irish funeral cloth used to drape a table holding the casket during home viewing. Beautifully stitched with cutwork and embroidery, it is a testimony to the love and respect held for loved ones.

49

shell of the loving father he had been. Time had run out before the necessary information had been provided.

It may be difficult to approach a parent and ask for basic personal information in order to help take care of their needs. A wise protective action plan for a caring child guardian would be to have the following information on a single piece of paper in a safe place or available through a lawyer or accountant. A safety deposit box at a bank is sealed once there is a death or an individual becomes incapacitated so this is not a good choice. Valuable time could be lost.

As parents ourselves, what about taking out a piece of paper to write down the information needed. Our children will be grateful. You may feel more comfortable leaving the paper with a lawyer or accountant, and let your children know the information is available in case it is needed.

Remember to update facts periodically as changes occur. A suggested list begins on the next page. Add your special requests.

Name

Address

Date/place born/birth certificate or where registered

Name of mother/father and where born

Social Security number

Insurance company, policy numbers
    and location of all policies

Banks

Special accounts

Charge card account names and numbers

Name of accountant (if any)

Name of lawyer (if any)

Location of important papers: will, home deed, car title

Family medical history (an important one)

Stars and Stripes, 16 x 22-inches

Many events begin with saluting the American flag. A flag quilt is a good design for a memorial to military persons. A collection of patriotic fabrics were assembled. All those stars and stripes beckoned one day while cutting out triangles.

The Santa figurine was made by fabric dressing over a ceramic base. Thomas Nast, a political cartoonist, first drew the Uncle Sam Santa as the cover of an 1863 Harpers Weekly magazine.

Discovering World Peace, 75 x 88-inches

This "world" quilt is an up-to-date variation of the Attic Windows. It was chosen as one of forty from around the world in a Quilter's Newsletter Magazine competition titled "Quilts: Discovering a New World." The circle rim behind the nine patch windows is ellusive much as world peace appears to be an ellusive dream. The quilt traveled to the Netherlands for the Quilt Expo display, as well as several sites in the states. The nine patch quilt design would be easy for you to experiment on.

In the loss of one partner of a couple, there is the loss of a life style that can be painful and requires adjustments. You are now the extra person, the odd one, or the fifth wheel; none of which is a comfortable place to be. The realignment of some friendships is obvious. A little thought from caring family and friends can ease the pain and stress. Let's look at the examples below.

Did the rules for bridge change? Joanne and Harold shared a great life together. They enjoyed bridge, walks in the woods, experimenting with new recipes, and life together. Their main social contacts with their friends, some from her college days, were playing cards and attending gourmet dinners.

Joanne passed away after a short illness. Imagine the void in Harold's life, plus most social contacts of the past were gone. Instantly! It takes two to play cards. A gradual separation of past friendships would help while new patterns of building a life take place.

Sharon was a part of a four couple group that did so many things together. She listened as a friend talked of the frustrations and loss of friendships after a separation. Why, that would never happen to her! These special lifelong friends would continue to be bosom buddies. After her husband died, Sharon could not believe that it happened to her. Can you imagine the pain she felt when it slipped out that there had been a holiday party. Without her!

Another group of friends faced the above problems differently. The emphasis of their activities changed focus to include their friend who needed the social contacts even more after a loss. Yes, many activities are couple oriented, but it does not take much creative planning to minimize the "couple" image. This allows a caring atmosphere which promotes healing.

Some activities, especially hobbies, are gender oriented. These contacts bring joy and a sharing of common interests. Quilters often express how much easier "the move to a new location was" because they knew a quilt guild would introduce them to new friends.

Common tasks can be overwhelming for one who has never had responsibility for them before. Cooking became a chore for John who had the problem of getting everything ready to eat at the same time. He found himself eating individual items as they were cooked. What a mess when the laundry overflowed at the same time he was trying to eat!

The car can be a frustrating responsibility for one who has never even pumped a tank of gas. Running out of gas is a real problem I can attest to.

Yard work overwhelmed Eleanor because of an obstinate or balky starting lawn mower. Imagine her surprise when a friend mowed her lawn once when she hadn't noticed the long grass. At first, she was upset that she had failed; chatting over glasses of ice tea when the lawn mowing was finished helped ease her frustrations.

Don't think in the terms of failure; we can't be expected to be good at all tasks. I write this down, yet find myself doing things that a helper would enjoy doing for me if only they had been given the opportunity.

Slip Through the Cracks, 21 x 29-inches

    The quilt has one square with all the other shapes circular. A person in grief may feel like they are slipping through the crack in the floor. Would it be that sometimes we feel out of place...a square in a world of circles? Notice how the quilting changes the images of the appliqued circles and square. A circle shape is quilted within the square, squares are quilted within the circles. This represents how fragile and changeable feelings are. With healing comes hope.

Drunkard's Path Sampler, 72 x 100-inches

The drunkard's path 4-inch square has a curve taken out of one corner. The way it is set together determines the name, i.e. Chain Path, Dirty Windows, Wonder of the World, Oregon Trail, Solomon's Puzzle, Love Ring. Curve stitching requires precision, but patience and practice help.

The path of losses associated with alcohol and "drunk" problems is enormous. Addiction causes losses that touch many parts of life just as this pattern represents many facets.

Chapter 6
Help! Where are the Words?

Whether a situation requires strength because of events happening to us or experienced by those close to us, we can prepare ourselves somewhat ahead of time. Find a verse, hymn, poem or short piece of literature that has comforting words. Memorize it so that it is always available when needed. The words in the Serenity Prayer have helped many accept the changes in their lives:

**God grant me the serenity to accept
the things I cannot change;
the courage to change the ones I can;
and the wisdom to know the difference.**

What can we say to acknowledge loss? It may be difficult to express our concern for those who are hurting. The words we express may seem inadequate. The important thing is that a gesture of care and love is expressed. Often the simpler the statement the better, such as "I'm sorry!" followed by a brief acknowledgement of specific loss. Be sensitive to the needs of the one who is suffering. A few minutes of conversation allows the loss to be discussed if the person needs someone to talk with.

A quick change of the subject may help the person expressing sorrow move to a more comfortable topic of conversation, but does not help the one dealing with a loss. In death situations, relating a specific memory you have of the person is usually comforting. In other losses, a good listener is needed to allow expressions of emotion. Just be available! Be comfortable with silence; your presence is what is important.

Phrases are often spoken without much meaning and may be interpreted as an empty gesture. There are some phrases we use in expressing comfort that may have an adverse effect. These thoughts may need to be worded differently to become more meaningful and less painful to the hurting individual.

Care expressed with the wrong words may be upsetting. For example, "I know exactly how you feel" is a common one. There are too many variable situations to know how another person feels. "Tell me how you feel" opens the door to communication.

For example, a friend commented to Roberta "You must be terribly lonely." This acknowledges an understanding by her, but it painfully brought out the feeling of loneliness. Maybe Roberta was actually feeling pretty good about some other aspect of life right then. Later reviewing the visit brought into focus just how lonely life had become.

Think how much more thoughtful the following comment would have been, "Let's have lunch tomorrow" or "I walk twice a week, would you join me one of those times next week?" This approach recognizes the problem; the difference is a solution was offered.

One day Marie decided to do something about the feeling of gloom that hung over her. She needed to

Morning Glory Fan Quilt, 58 x 86-inches

This quilt was acquired suddenly while talking with my hands to a friend at a quilt auction! The 1930's Japanese Fans were overpowered by the blue sashing. An idea came. Morning glory vines and flowers were appliqued up the sashing; they were positioned to cover a couple of worn spots. New life was restored or a quilt was recycled! Do our flaws, worn spots and sharp edges show? The sharp edges of pain do round out with time. Kindness and genuine expressions of concern help.

Memorial to Dad and Mom

Men's ties allow them to make a fashion statement, both in color and design. Ties would make a great fan block to frame; even a whole quilt of fan blocks. The bow tie is another way to honor the special men in your life. The heart shaped miniature wall quilt piece has bow tie blocks set diagonally across the piece. Be sure to indicate whose ties they were, and who made the quilt.

For Mom or a favorite aunt, you may choose to preserve a beautiful hankie with lace edging. Add a pastel fan, and frame.

communicate with someone. Marie decided to invite an elderly couple for dinner. Grocery shopping for special foods made the outing fun over routine shopping for one. Besides, there were people to chat with. Fixing dinner, baking a fresh strawberry sour cream pie, and setting the table made for a busy afternoon. The best part was the dinner conversation for Marie as the couple enjoyed sharing stories.

Pride can get in the way of an easier time for us. Asking for help is very difficult for most folks. It is much easier for most of us to be givers, graciousness is in being able to receive when the need arises. People are generous, well meaning and caring.

Words need to transfer from the person in need to the available source of aid. Sally offered a ride if her friend would just call her. Her friend has to take the first step to ask for help, swallow her pride or whatever it takes to make that move. She should remember how good it made her feel when she was able to help others at a different time in life. Sally, who is sincere in helping a friend, needs to feel wanted.

Over and over we are cared for in spite of our pride. This was the case when arriving home one evening with heavy shipping cases to be removed from the car. A neighbor happened along! The heavy cases were carried and conversation welcomed home a weary traveller. The importance of "conversation" changed the scene from one of despair to a lightened load.

In other words, the opportunity to be in service to our neighbor is provided by simply asking. We may remember if we think of how labels affect the thought process...like calling milk that has soured, spoiled; soured milk is also called sour cream, a product that is very useful. The label of care giver often proves as beneficial to the care giver as it does to the person being cared for.

As long as Heather can get to the computer, she is in communication with other quilters across the country in one of the on-line programs. Her quilt guild is nationwide, not just in the community. Modern technology has extended our support network. Many use this means for their contact with the outside world during times of limited participation.

Stitchers are ready to communicate through the keyboard to help each other work through the problems faced by the fictitious presence behind the call name on the screen. Quilt problems are discussed and emotional care is given.

Words from others do help. What if the hurt is just too deep for us to express the feelings through communicating with another? This may be the time to take out pen and paper and start writing the words down. There may be letters that need to be sent, words that need to be spoken, and thoughts that no longer can be communicated.

It can be healing therapy to write these words down to remove the chains, guilt, roadblocks, and carry-over hangups that keep dragging us down. Give these away by writing out the words. If possible to send to help rebuild relationships, consider it. Or just the fact of

The Star Oak, 88 x 99--inches

Many antique quilts were made by using four large blocks. These were often set together with a secondary design filling in the areas around the stars. Autumn colors for the Diamond Starburst lone star variation suggested the oak leaf with acorns. The straight lines of the star were softened with curved applique. Linda's granddaughter picked a star in the sky when she wanted to talk to her Granny. Children feel the changes in life, yet process them at their level.

Autumn Star, 88 x 98-inches

The Autumn Star quilt was planned on a drive through a northern state where the leaves of the maples and other trees turn brilliant colors. It is not necessary to make quilts like traditional ones were made or even like a pattern suggests. The eight pointed star is made of dark diamonds with a light background. Most shaded quilts are done in squares, which are easier to piece. The star pattern pieces were more challenging. Be creative...march to your own drummer!

relieving us of the burden may open door to better understanding ourselves.

Communicating with others is a need most of us share. Well chosen words can be very healing. Listening is considered more important than words. Words followed by actions are the key to building a life as well as making a creative project. We can move up the ladder to a successful quilt or lifestyle by adding our own words to the children's story of the little train that kept trying.

I won't call for a ride,
I can't swallow my pride.
I don't know how to piece the block,
I wish I could beat the clock.
I think I might start today
I think I can learn to say
I did make it!

Henry Ford put it another way, "Whether you think you can or think you can't, you're right."

Jacob's Ladder

Chapter 7
Return to Creative Life

All that has happened to us in life becomes a part of our inner being and affects our creative endeavors. We may expect to see changes in the colors we use. Often the darker hues used following a change become brighter once healing time has elapsed. Stitchers use their needlework skills to express what is happening at the time.

Let's look at several cases of how loss affects our sense of well being enough to change our creative habits. Most often the sudden loss jolts us to the very core. Even expected losses require our inner strength. There needs to be time taken to deal with a loss. The body may heal rather quickly. However, the emotional inner being usually takes much longer.

Time is required elsewhere; time that once was spent on creative outlets such as quiltmaking, art, music, cooking or gardening. Even if time is not the factor, it can be the thought process that still is required to work through questions that are left unanswered.

Yes, we can and are required to go back to work just a few days after a personal loss. Andrew returned to school to face finals the week after his Dad died, having missed a week of preparatory classes. We function, but the loss leaves its imprint taking its toll on our thought process and energy. The loss of energy being used to process the mind's inner working thoughts are difficult to explain to those who have not experienced it.

Trip Around the World, 20 x 20-inch quilt, 12-inch doll

A quilt made of squares with color waves moving out from center is called Trip Around the World. We traded artistic talents by each making two, one to give and one to keep. The same print fabric was used in both. The doll was made by dollmaker Suzie Robinson, Peddlers of Danville. Handmade dolls are special to little children. Things that happen in childhood affect us throughout life. We continue to learn how important those early years are.

Ballerina Graduation Recital, 62 x 86-inches

Squares made into nine patch blocks make a great background to interpret a silhouette idea. Lightly shaded nine patch blocks form a shimmery background for ballerina applique. A rose is at the ballerina's feet. The block row around the nine patch stage is much darker, followed by a row of medium blocks. The accumulated leftover squares became the final three rows for a border frame. It is important to honor our children's accomplishments. This quilt was a hit at college.

The changes in our lives often leave us no time for former activities, whether they were necessary or just for fun. The time factor takes over especially if activities are in the hobby field. For many, the craft/art area of our life suffers to the point that it affects other areas of life.

Norma was prolific in the almost masterpiece quilts she designed and made for a number of years. Suddenly shocked by the news that her husband was leaving she found her life a complete upheaval. The energy it takes to be creative was now spent in being a single parent, finding a new home, and generally dealing with the changes life had brought. The changes had been thrust upon her without any warning, but more importantly without any decision on her part.

Norma's quiltmaking had been the artistic joy that fed her soul. We talked about the need to be creative, to express oneself in a medium that once had brought so much joy to life. As time healed and the pieces began to fall into place with other parts of her life, the creative side simply was not there. She felt an important part of her identity had been lost. Where had it gone? How long before the creative side of life would return? What can be done to regain a creative spirit which was lost?

Patsy, a quilter who has a debilitating condition which causes both physical and emotional difficulties, expresses the different peaks and valleys she faces. When the disease takes over and the body seems out of control, the depth of depression becomes the valley to get through. The only area where she can predict the outcome is her patchwork. In other words, it is time for straight patchwork piecing of squares, rectangles or triangles. Time for paper piecing...a technique where fabric is attached to the exact size paper pattern to assure accuracy. The pieces going together form a whole design giving hope there is more order predictable in what is happening.

A change occurs when the disease is in remission and there can be a return to a more artistic time. During this period the mind is freed from the burden of pain and some of the added medication. Patsy is able to be more creative. Curves appear and free flowing designs come with ease.

This quilter uses the art of quiltmaking both as therapy in the valleys and soars with it to the mountain top during remission. Another aspect of her stitchery is that patchwork becomes a means of communicating with the medical staff on a lighter side. She is sharing a part of herself.

Some Ways to Regain Creativity ... Jump start the imagination!

1. Change your routine.
2. Look at something different today. Go to a museum, an art exhibit, or choose some other means of feeding the creative process.
3. Look at things through the eyes of a child; total simplicity just as it is without any of the nets, safety glasses, or hangups we adults often attach.
4. Get in touch with your inner self. Find peace of mind to allow it to be receptive to new thoughts and ideas.

Virginia Cardinal and Dogwood, 15 x 36-inches

    The frame was made of a barn board that was shaped with a roof line peak. The lumber was cut on my Granddad's farm in Virginia for Dad when it was time for him to build a barn. As the barn was raised for the development of home sites, saving a part of my heritage was important. I made similar pieces for my sister and both brothers. The Virginia state flower and bird seemed an appropriate design to put in the oval cut out shape. See the dogwood pattern on pages 44-45 and learn to applique.

Country Roads to City Streets, 36 x 36-inches

Neighborhoods change right before our very eyes. We often see the lush green of the country where the roads are few and far apart disappear. In its place appear lots of cement, homes, and other buildings, with their multi-lane city streets. The loss of trees is illustrated by the lifeless tree standing silhouetted against the city scape. If you look closely, you will see that the design is made of nine patch blocks with three strips as sashing between blocks. Quilts, like other works of art, have stories to tell.

Pause and take inventory.
5. Daydream in technicolor. Surround yourself with colors if you are a quiltmaker, music if you are a musician, flowers if a gardner.
6. Take time to be in a creative spirit with a day off, or even an hour. Find time where there is none, for example driving time.
7. Find a friend with whom to share your interest.

Roadblocks to a Creative Spirit
1. Fatigue
2. Emotional upheaval
3. A place to work (yes, work for some, play for others)
4. Lack of a realistic goal
5. A timetable for completion.

Believe in yourself, never say never; for you can do just about whatever you set out to do. And presto! As healing occurs and the adjustments to the changes come into focus, sparks of your former creative self begin to ignite new ideas and projects. What has happened will most likely be reflected in the new work, for we are a cumulative resource of all that has been put into our inner self. In other words, we are seasoned by our sorrows. As a result, our creativity gains depth and meaning. A new you is evolving!

Like many artistic forms, quiltmaking is a self-expression of feelings and emotions. Read some of the stories on the making of the pieces photographed for the book to check out the theory. You may find it helpful to use quilting as a means of working through life changes.

Quilting can be looked at as a product producer or as an art process. Is it art or craft? The answer is both. We need quilts for warmth, but they can be beautifully artistic. A fiber artist that uses the quilt medium for producing art objects for the wall would be insulted if her prize piece was considered a blanket for warmth.

Do something artistic for your mental and emotional health. You may need to throw away the time spent. Sometimes throw away the memory of dollars spent for extra fat quarters of fabric (or yards) required to gain a palette of color in which to work.

The opposite may test you to be creative with what is available. Make a decision on a design you have seen in a pattern book, or start with pencil, paper and eraser. Don't get caught up in the end result, but enjoy the therapeutic value creativity offers to enrich life. Sometimes it can truly be a lifesaver!

Every great task begins with a vision, followed by a detailed plan or sketch of the vision. Consult the sketch to double check along the way, but be flexible to what the fabrics and colors say. Often times changes need to be made; take a different road to reach the final outcome. There is great joy when the photograph develops to let us see the accomplishment of our labors. Find someone with whom to share the excitement of accomplishment.

Quiltmaking can be a long and tedious task depending on the complexity of the design. Therefore, don't wait until the completion to celebrate. Find milestones along

Paths of Wedded Love, 36 x 36 and 10-1/2 x 14-inches

I was invited to make a Silver Dollar City challenge piece using the theme of "Fun and Romance in America's Past." The double wedding ring is such a recognized pattern; the quilt won viewer's choice. Memories of mothers, grandmothers or a favorite aunt quiltmaker come to mind. The strip pieced variation above divides the center of the ring to give a diagonal look. A heart was appliqued in the plain area. Off center quilt art has become more popular. Begin a family heirloom today.

Home and Heart, 32 x 51-inches

Nine two story house blocks are combined with six shaded heart blocks. Note the heart appliqued above the doors of the houses. There are a number of house blocks. One is called a schoolhouse block.

The importance of love in the home is expressed in this wall quilt. It would also make a good crib quilt. Take a photo of your favorite home to study. Enlarge it for a pattern to make a block to preserve that part of your life.

the way. A youngster was overheard telling his friend who was all excited about the quilt his Mom was making, "it would be three years before he would have it 'caus that's jest how long it takes."

Be penny-wise and pound foolish in the selection process both of design and color. Too complicated a design drags on and dampens the spirit...definitely something that is not called for while life is presenting its own challenges. We may not be able to look for instant success; there is merit in working to achieve a completed project. The journey is part of the goal.

By experimenting you will discover your design potential or select a pattern from one of the many quilt books. Most everyone has more creative ability than they are willing to admit. Expect to be successful. In the planning stages keep in mind there has to be a balance between difficulty, available time and your skill level.

Experiment with color. Your personal preferences for decorating or the clothes you wear can give clues to what appeals to your color sense. Observe and check eye appeal! Are you a bright color or pastel individual? Does the color emphasis of your area of the country enter into the decision process? By experimenting you will discover your design potential.

Think of the colored fabric you have chosen for a project as your palette of paints. Do you have a good variety that is pleasing to the eye? Do any of the fabric colors stand out from all the others or become the first thing you see? Disturbing? Or, could this fabric be a highlight spark of interest that adds a touch of excitement to the design?

The piece will be more interesting if the print fabrics have varying size designs on them. For example, even a well planned quilt could be boring if all the fabrics are small print floral calicos. The same might be true when using all large print fabrics. Work toward collecting a pleasant mix.

Machine versus hand work is a decision to consider. Machine work can speed along the stitching. If life is on the quiet side, if too much thinking time can get to you, then the sewing machine could be just the answer. At other times it is difficult to face the noisy machine after tedious hours of work. Hand stitching can be a relaxing change of pace.

Have you thought about doing a piece where nature becomes the design master? Leaves and flowers may be laid on a copy machine to give that realistic shape for applique work. You may even decide to arrange a grouping of flowers and leaves. If the flower is white or pastel, a dark sheet of paper is needed to cover it so the design shows. Be sure to clean away any residue before the next paper goes on copier.

Other artistic sources help those of us who say we can't draw a flower or floral arrangement. Wall paper books are wonderful sources for ideas. Select a design from a pattern book in a different technique than you have done before; take a class to familiarize yourself with something new. The freshness of a new pattern or technique adds interest. A class offers a sharing time with others.

Sunrise Cross, 24 x 32"-inches

The Guiding Star, a Kansas City Star newspaper design from 1933, makes a perfect block for a cross. Dark fabric forms the cross, gold is for the sunrise feeling. A stripe fabric was over dyed to frame the cross before adding blue fill-in fabric to make the rectangle shape. Greeting cards for the Easter season provided the idea for quilting lilies in the blue area.

The "Guiding Star" seemed appropriate. The cross and Easter symbolize death and a new life God shares with us.

Maybe you are a quilter who likes to piece the geometric designs. These may be set next to each other to achieve those secondary patterns that add another whole dimension to the quilt. Or divide the blocks with sashing to highlight each block. Makes fewer blocks go further! You be the decision maker to determine your quilt design...or the shape life takes.

The folk art of quilting has continued over the years because it is such a symbol of a gift of love combined with sharing and caring. As a quiltmaker, I dwell in a land of creativity, often seeing the world through rose colored glasses. Reality forces removal of the glasses to see what the day holds.

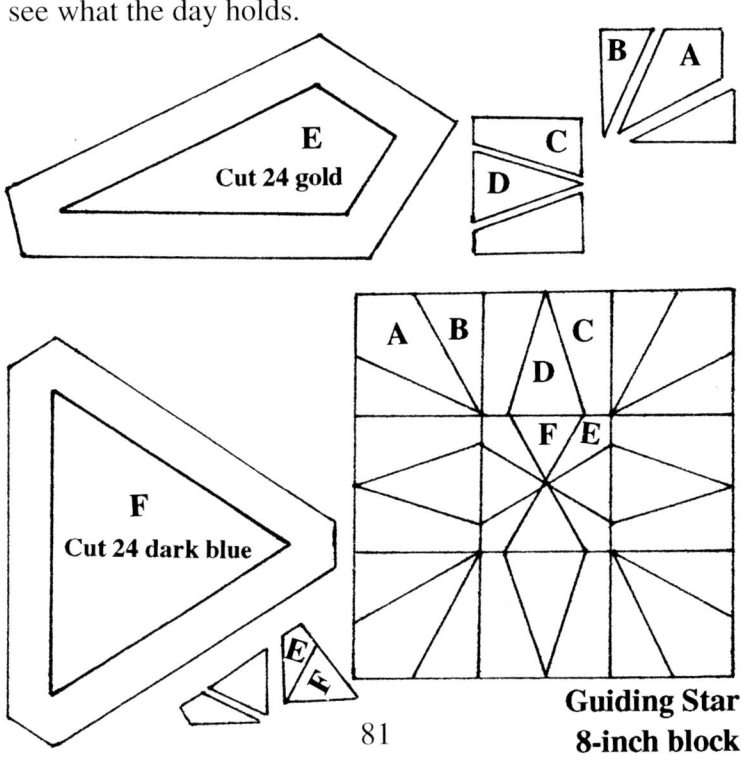

E
Cut 24 gold

F
Cut 24 dark blue

**Guiding Star
8-inch block**

D
Cut 24 dark blue

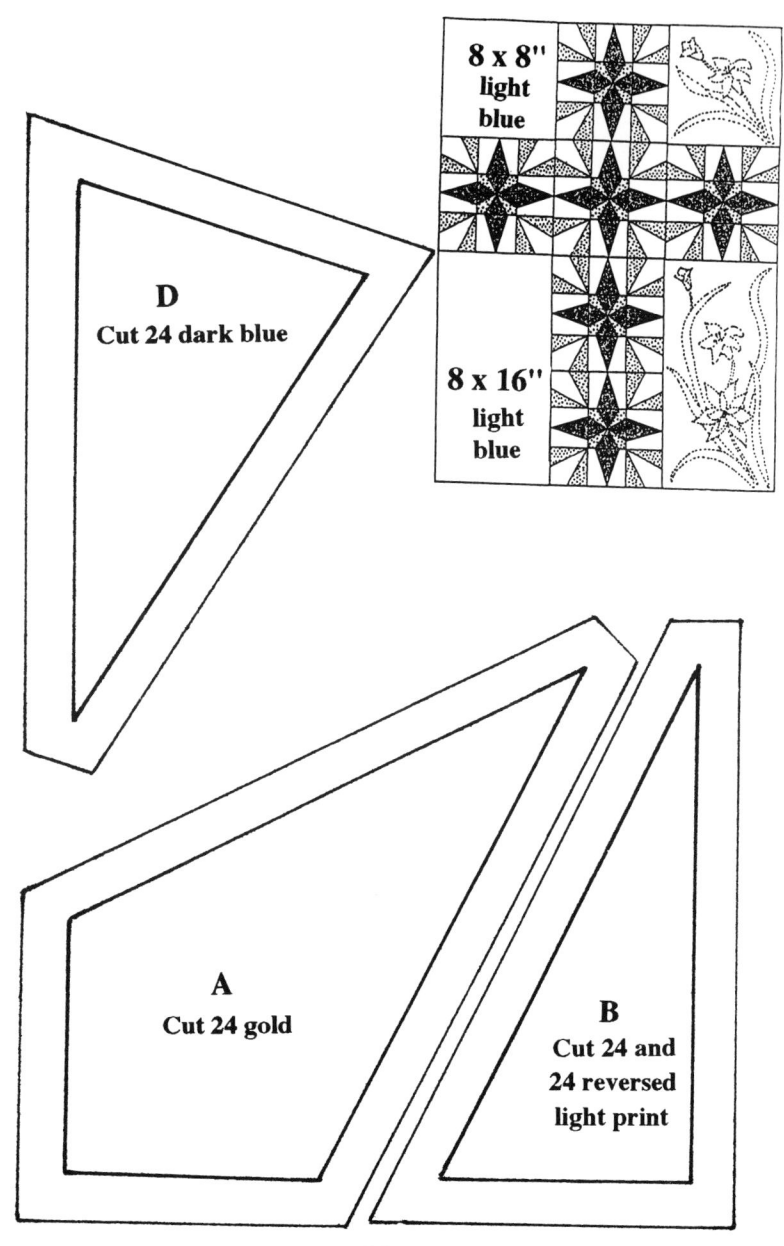

8 x 8" light blue

8 x 16" light blue

A
Cut 24 gold

B
Cut 24 and 24 reversed light print

82

The Guiding Star was a delight to work with. It was one of the 98 different stars from my book, Star Quest for Quilters. The book also includes the same block in a 12-inch size pattern which would make the quilt 40 x 52-inches.

The Guiding Star block might look difficult, but when you break it down there are just three separate units that make up a nine patch block. See the piecing guide. The actual pattern is a darker line, with the 1/4-inch seam allowance a lighter line. Piece six blocks. The width of the border stripe for the star will be determined by the fabric you choose. The measurements for the light blue fill-in fabric are in the quilt sketch (add seam allowance).

Trace the pattern. Piece blocks, set together so that the stripe frame may be cut and pieced around the star. If using a stripe fabric, it is important to miter the corners so that the stripes match. May we say that is the difference between "handmade" and "homemade". Set in light blue to make a rectangle shape. Mark your quilting design. Quilt and bind off. A 4-inch hanging sleeve sewn on the back makes it easy to slip a rod through for hanging.

Fabric Requirements: 3 yards light blue (includes binding and backing), 1/4 yard dark blue, 1/4 yard white, 1/4 yard light print, 1/3 yard gold. It will take 3-1/2 yards stripe (this is not yards of fabric, but yards of actual stripe).

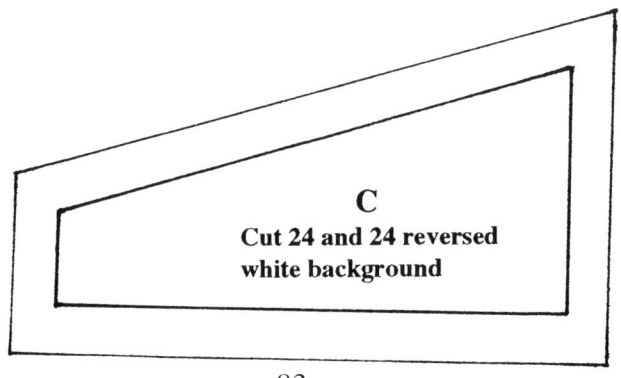

C
Cut 24 and 24 reversed
white background

Chapter 8
Piecing My Life Together

Julie Andrews as Maria in the Sound of Music stated as she left the safety of the nuns in the Abbey, "When the Lord closes the door, somehow he opens a window." It is called hope. Just as small bits and pieces of fabric go together to form a whole, the remnants of our lives begin to mend. With time, the events take their place.

When our spirits are broken and we are going through the valley of the shadow of death, both our inner frailties and resources become exposed. We are opened up for others to move in to help with the healing process.

As a quilter and teacher of quilting, my goal is to experiment with patterns, colors and designs to pass along what I have learned. In this way, projects are easier for others because of my experimenting.

The events of last few months caught me off guard because of the suddenness; age was a factor too. Once I started writing thoughts down, one big question kept me resisting. Why? Would it help me to write about these months? Could I? Or were the emotions still too painful? Would readers gain from comments shared by others? Each person's experiences, feelings and losses are so individualized. Would my writing help others prepare?

In the early days, taking notes while reading helped the message be absorbed when the mind was not functioning. Even right in the middle of a conversation, a memory might cross the brain waves to race the mind off on a different thought. Concentration was missing.

Cooking had been second nature. Food preparation became such a chore with very little success. It would take extra trips to the grocery store to pick up forgotten items. The golden brown of baked goods had become dark bronze. With time, skills gradually returned.

Holidays were days to get through, not anticipated. Our usual 8-foot Christmas tree now is small enough for me to lift, set up and take down. The traditional ornaments have stayed packed away because of too many memories. A dozen white doves were all the decorations that went on the tree the first year. The second year tree was decorated with a collection of Santa ornaments for the grandchildren's eyes. That was progress!

I have learned to avoid times that have potential for despair by planning something...like anniversaries and special event dates. It helps, but I realize one can still feel alone even in a crowded room. Life is not taken for granted. I have learned to appreciate the simple joys.

I have come full circle in dealing with a lot of issues related to the loss of loved ones and readjustment to life. And only part way round the circle in other areas. How long before the answer to a "How are you?" greeting will be "fine" with sincerity and honesty? It has moved up to "Okay" as a respectable substitute.

It is difficult to change from "our" and "we" to "my" and "I". When you hear a person use the plural form, think with me of we as God, family and friends in an all encompassing way. It prevents a feeling of standing alone against the world...and the pieces come together.

Bibliographical References

Brothers, Dr. Joyce (1990), Widowed, "dedicated to every woman and every man who has lost a dearly beloved person...whether to death of the body or death of love," Joyce B. Enterprises, Inc.

Buscaglia, Leo (1982), the Fall of Freddie the Leaf, a Story of Life for All Ages, Charles B.Slack,Inc., Holt, Rinehart and Winston.

Cornils, Stanley P. (1967), Managing Grief Wisely, Baker Book House, Grand Rapids, Michigan.

Curry, Cathleen L. (1993), When Your Parent Dies, A concise and practical source of help and advice for adults grieving the death of a parent., Ave Marie Press, Notre Dame, Indiana 46556.

Grollman, Earl A. (1977), Living When a Loved One Has Died, Beacon Press, Boston, Massachusetts

Hospice, National Hospice Organization, 1901 North Moore Street, Suite 901, Arlington, VA 22209 (703-243-5900 or 800-658-8898 for information about Hospice care and referral to Hospice programs throughout the U.S.)

James, John W. and Frank Cherry, (1988) The Grief Recovery Handbook, A Step-by-Step Program for Moving Beyond Loss, Harper & Row, New York, NY.

Lewis, C. S. (March 1976), A Grief Observed, A Masterpiece of Rediscovered Faith, Bantam Book, published by arrangement with the Seabury Press.

O'Toole, Donna (1993), Healing and Growing Through Grief, Mountain Rainbow Publications, 477 Hannah Branch Road, Burnsville, NC 28714

Rupp, Joyce (1988), Praying Our Goodbyes, Ave Marie Press, Notre Dame, Indiana, 46556.

Westberg, Granger E. (1962, 1971), Good Grief, A Constructive Approach to the Problem of Loss, Fortress Press, Philadelphia.

Worden, J. William (1991), Grief Counseling & Grief Therapy, A Handbook for the Mental Health Practitioner, Springer Publishing Co., 536 Broadway, New York, NY 10012-3955.

Yeagley, Larry (1981, 1984) Grief Recovery, Seventh Day Adventist Church, 1055 Horton Road, Muskegon, MI 49445

Your Notes

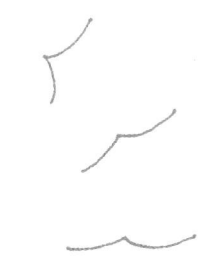

My Notes:
Not everyone's attic windows are the same size! A quilting tradition says you should never make a perfect quilt, for only God is perfect. Did you notice the far left two rows of the cover quilt? Let me explain. The eleven rows had been done earlier, the template misfiled, and the final two rows were made from different size templates for the square. I was intent on the color choices and did not notice the change in size. Remember reading about lack of concentration during stressful times. No need to worry about a perfect quilt this time!

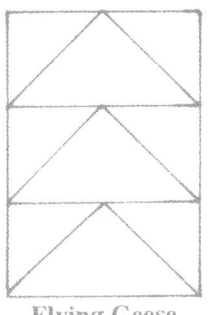

Flying Geese